AF235595

Ricky Roogle

Crewmate Notebook

NOT AN OFFICIAL INNERSLOTH PRODUCT. NOT APPROVED BY OR ASSOCIATED WITH INNERSLOTH.

Bibliografische Information der Deutschen Nationalbibliothek:
Die Deutsche Nationalbibliothek verzeichnet diese Publikation in der
Deutschen Nationalbibliografie; detaillierte bibliografische
Daten sind im Internet über http://dnb.dnb.de abrufbar.

© 2021 Ricky Roogle; 1. Auflage
Covergraphic, text & illustrations © 2021 Ricky Roogle
contact author: ricky.roogle@t-online.de
Herstellung und Verlag: BoD – Books on Demand, Norderstedt
ISBN: 9783752658187